How do we KNOW About DINOSAURS?

A Fossil Mystery

by Rebecca Olien
Illustrated by Katie McDee

Consultant:
Mathew J. Wedel, PhD
Paleontologist and Assistant Professor
Western University of Health Sciences
Pomona, California

CAPSTONE PRESS
a capstone imprint

First Graphics are published by Capstone Press,
1710 Roe Crest Drive, North Mankato, Minnesota 56003.
www.capstonepub.com

Library of Congress Cataloging-in-Publication Data
Olien, Rebecca.
  How do we know about dinosaurs? : a fossil mystery / by Rebecca Olien ;
illustrated by Katie McDee.
      p. cm.—(First graphics. Science mysteries)
  Includes bibliographical references and index.
  Summary: "In graphic novel format, text and illustrations explain how fossils
teach us about the dinosaurs"—Provided by publisher.
  ISBN 978-1-4296-6095-2 (library binding)
  ISBN 978-1-4296-7173-6 (paperback)
  1. Dinosaurs—Juvenile literature. 2. Fossils—Juvenile literature. 3. Graphic
novels—Juvenile literature. I. McDee, Katie, ill. II. Title. III. Series.
  QE861.5.O48 2012
  567.9—dc22   2011001013

EDITOR: CHRISTOPHER L. HARBO
DESIGNER: LORI BYE
ART DIRECTOR: NATHAN GASSMAN
PRODUCTION SPECIALIST: ERIC MANSKE

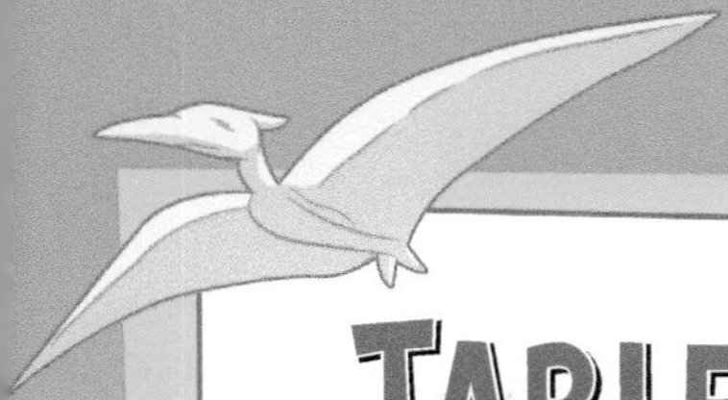

Table of Contents

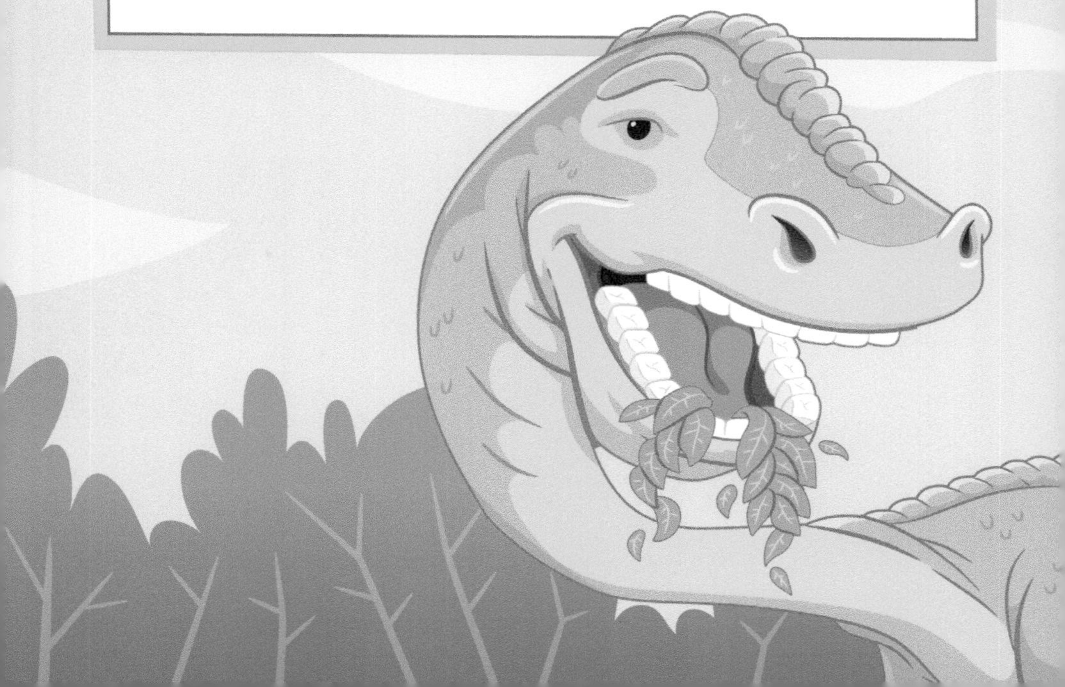

HAVE YOU EVER SEEN A GIANT DINOSAUR?

You can look, but you will never find a giant living dinosaur.

Dinosaurs in movies look alive. But they're not real.

The last giant dinosaurs lived millions of years before people were on Earth.

How do we know about dinosaurs?

How Do We Know Dinosaurs Lived?

We know dinosaurs lived from fossils. Fossils are the remains of plants and animals, preserved as rock.

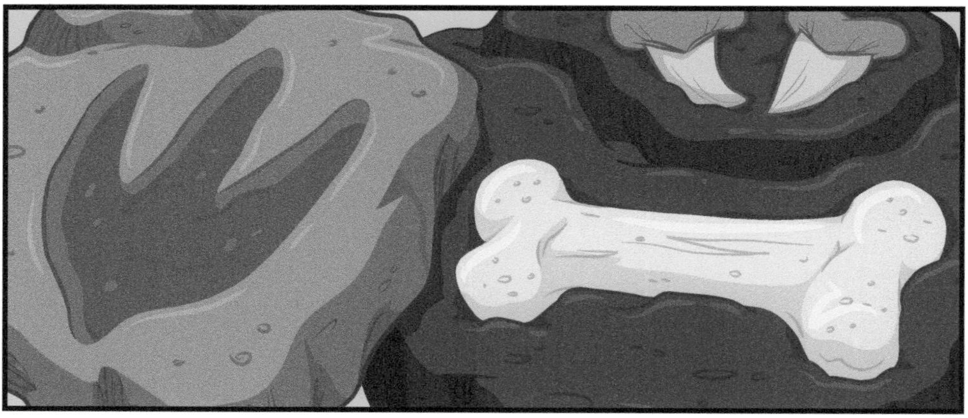

Scientists study fossils.

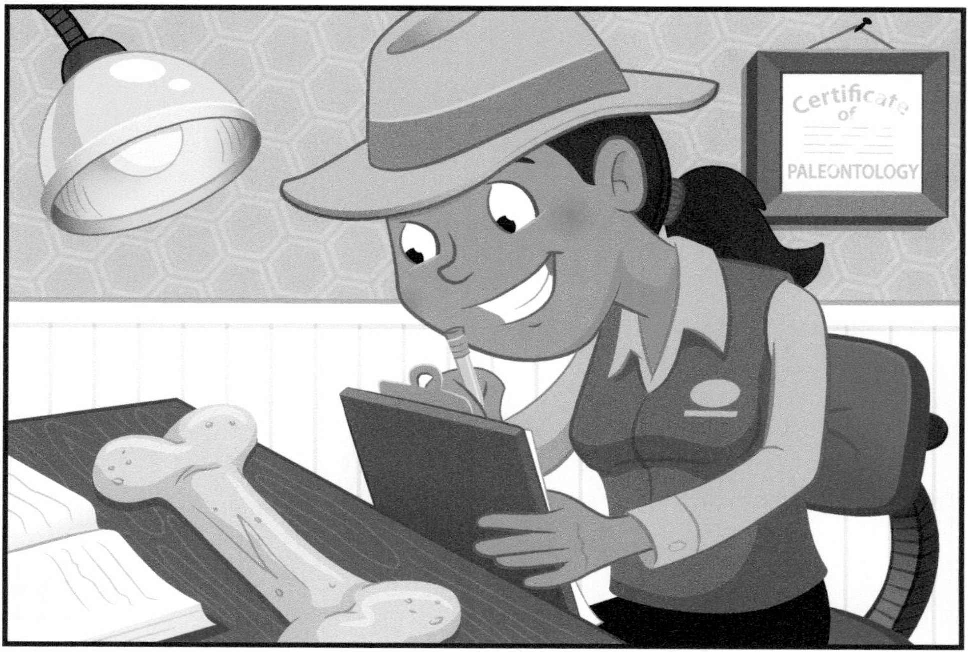
Certificate
of
PALEONTOLOGY

They look at each fossil to find clues about dinosaurs.

Fossils tell us everything we know about dinosaurs.

Not all dinosaurs became fossils. Most were eaten.
Some died and rotted away.

But some dinosaur bones did turn into fossils.
Here's how. This T-Rex died in a flood.

Mud buried its body. Its soft body parts rotted away.

Over time, the mud hardened into rock. The bones became fossils.

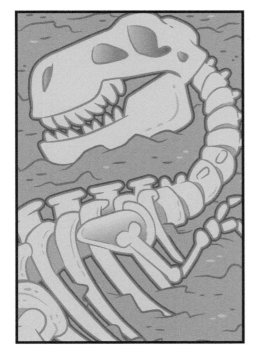

HOW ARE FOSSILS FOUND?

Over millions of years, the rock around a fossil wears away. Sometimes fossils are found by accident.

Other times, scientists hunt for fossils.

When they find fossils, scientists set up a dig site.
Workers carefully remove rock around fossils.

Workers pack small bones in crates. Large bones are
covered in plaster.

The fossils are taken to a science lab. Lab workers unpack the crates. They cut away the plaster.

Each fossil is cleaned.

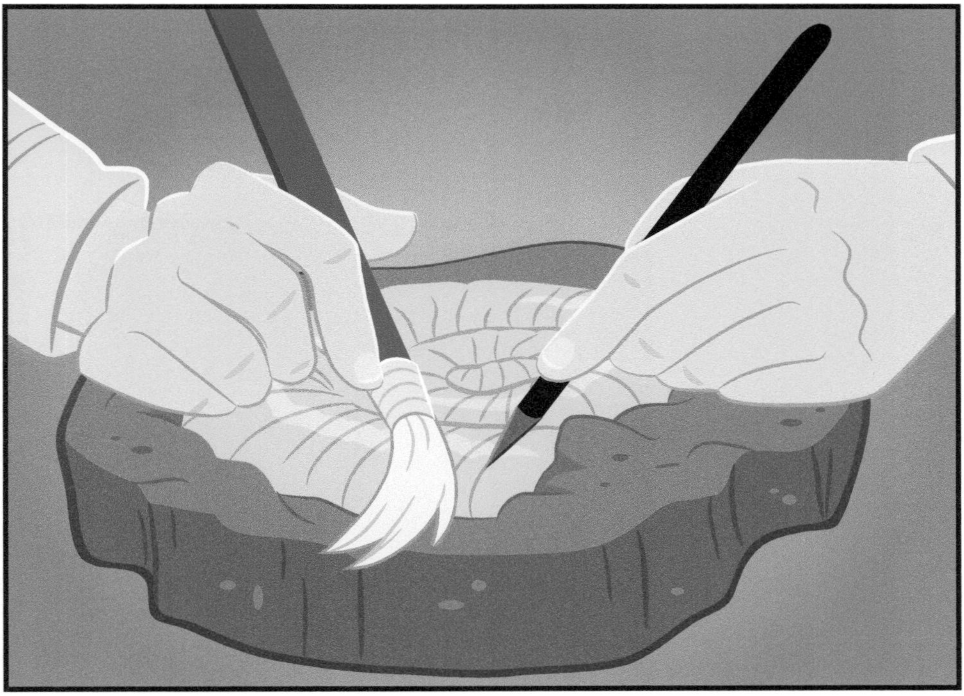

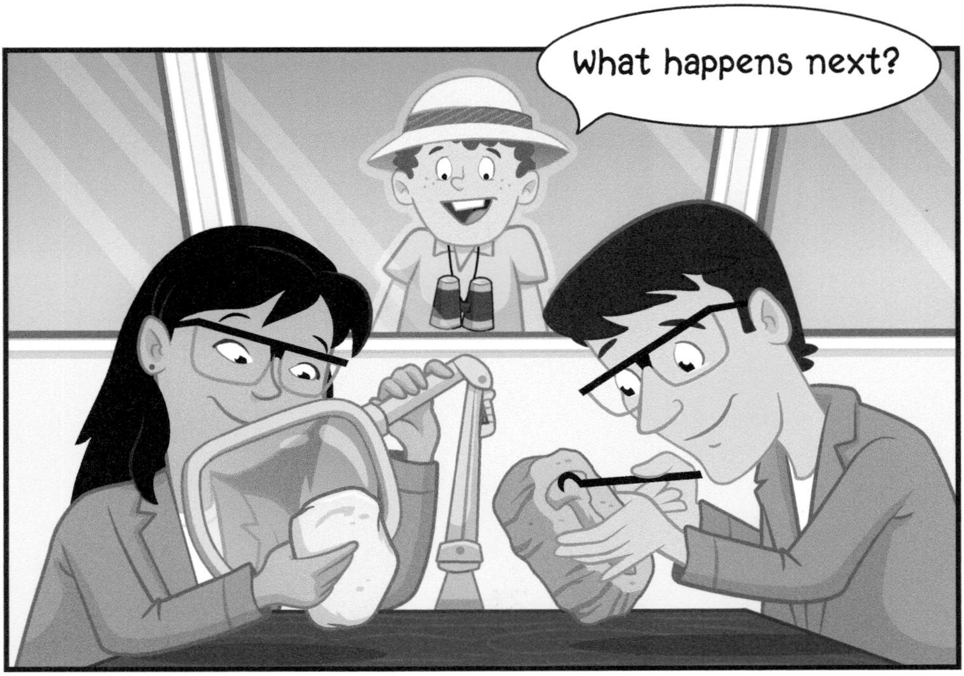
What happens next?

Sometimes scientists find enough bones to build a dinosaur skeleton.

Lab workers make plastic casts of each bone. These models look just like the real bones.

Scientists put the casts together to make a skeleton.

People visit museums to see the skeletons.

What Can We Learn from Dinosaur Fossils?

Fossils give us many clues about dinosaurs.
Teeth tell us what dinosaurs ate.

Flat teeth are for chewing plants.

Sharp teeth belong to meat eaters.

Even dinosaur droppings give us clues. Droppings full of bones show a dinosaur ate meat.

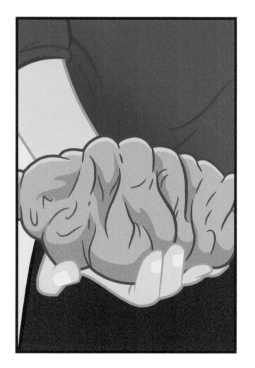

Fossils of nests show that dinosaurs hatched from eggs.

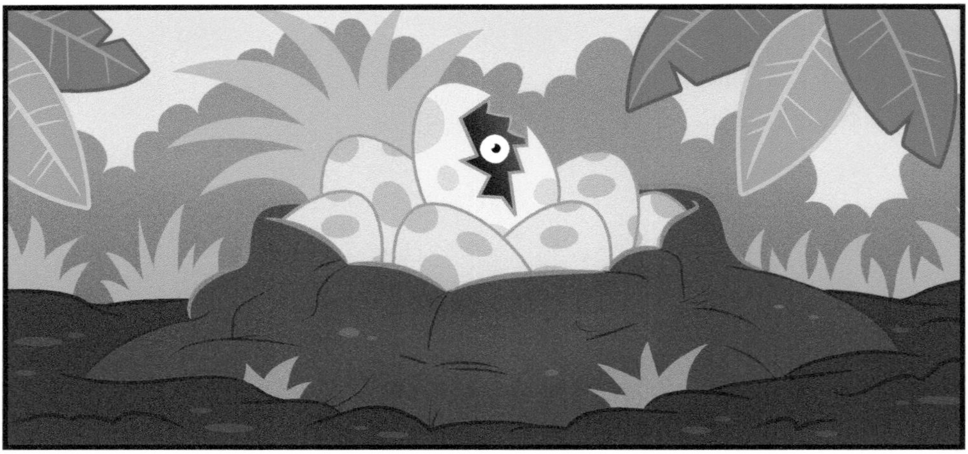

Footprint fossils give clues about a dinosaur's size.

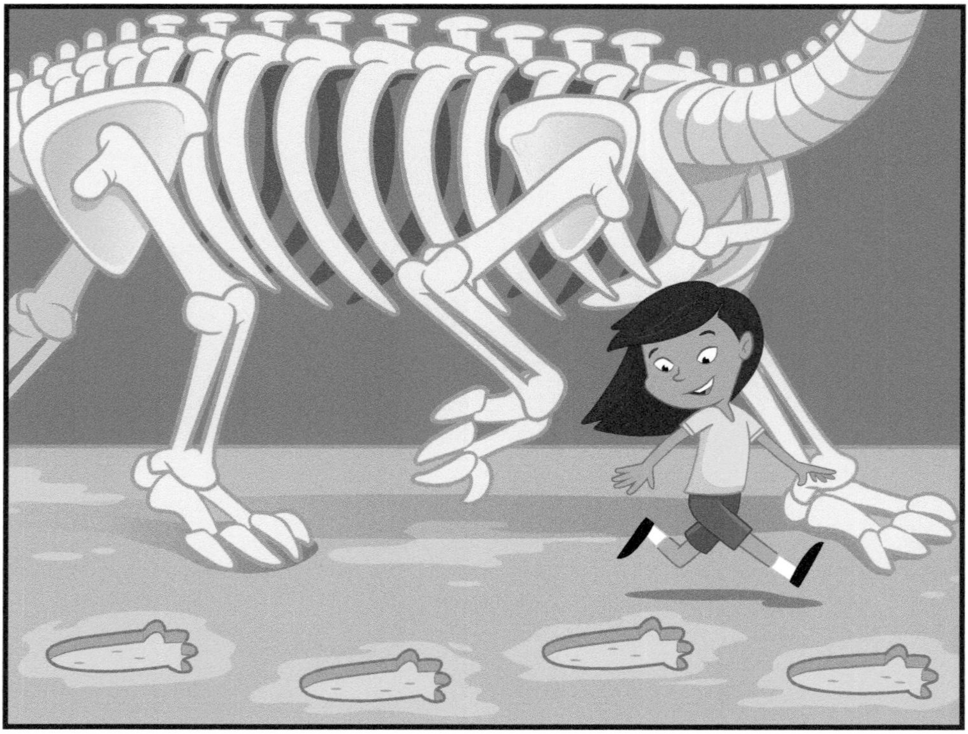

Sets of footprints show how some dinosaurs walked together.

Can I find dinosaur fossils too?

Anyone can find dinosaur fossils.

Dinosaur fossils have been found all over the world.

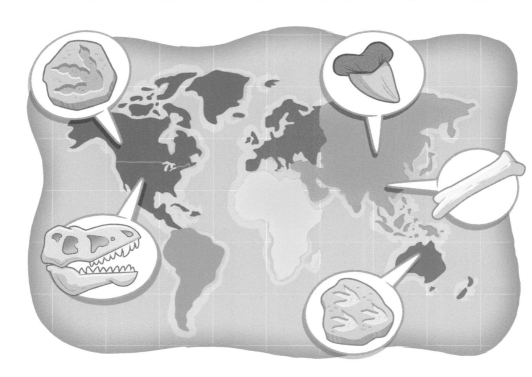

If you find a fossil, take a picture of it. Show the picture to a scientist at a museum.

Someday you might find a fossil that solves part of the dinosaur mystery.

GLOSSARY

cast—a model of something made of metal, plastic, or plaster

fossil—the remains or traces of an animal or a plant, preserved as rock

museum—a place where objects of art, history, or science are shown

mystery—something that is hard to explain or understand

plaster—a mixture of lime, sand, and water that dries hard

remains—parts of something that was once alive

skeleton—a framework of bones in a body

READ MORE

Naish, Darren. *Dinosaurs Life Size.* Hauppauge, N.Y.: Barrons Educational Series, Inc., 2010.

Olien, Rebecca. *What Happened to the Dinosaurs?: A Book About Extinction.* Why in the World. Mankato, Minn: Capstone Press, 2007.

Thomson, Sarah L. *Extreme Dinosaurs! Q & A.* New York: Collins, 2007.

INTERNET SITES

FactHound offers a safe, fun way to find Internet sites related to this book. All of the sites on FactHound have been researched by our staff.

Here's all you do:

Visit *www.facthound.com*

Type in this code: 9781429660952

Check out projects, games and lots more at
www.capstonekids.com

INDEX